Praise for *The Novel Ed.*

"This is the second time Kris Spisak has written a book that's helped my career. She asks the hard questions that authors need on the path from idea to publication, while respecting your unique method of thinking and writing. Spisak understands that writing is work, but it doesn't have to be a disorganized grind — and this book gave me a framework I could use to edit faster, more accurately, and in ways I hadn't considered. Get this book. Make a list. Get rid of "suddenly" in your manuscript. You'll thank Kris for all three and become a better writer."

-Author of thirty-two novels, Terry Maggert

"Kris Spisak brings her signature wit and can-do spirit to this guide brimming with practical, hands-on advice. From big picture restructuring to line-editing polish, Spisak's suggestions will help both the novice and the already-published revise their next manuscript and make it shine. A must-read and a fun read!"

-A.B. Westrick, author of *Brotherhood*

"Moving from the triumphant mess of a first draft to a polished and publishable finished product can challenge even the most experienced writer. And as a teacher of writing, helping students to understand the how to's of revision, especially for long works, is equally complicated. Author Kris Spisak has written a book that offers a welcome hand. With her confident and optimistic tone, Spisak is the writing coach we all want beside us as we tackle what can seem an impossible task. So whether you are a seasoned novelist or just starting out and trying to complete your first book, *The Novel Editing Workbook* is an invaluable tool to have at your side."

-Novelist, Essayist, and Creative Writing Teacher, Patricia A. Smith

The Novel Editing Workbook

105 Tricks & Tips for Revising Your Fiction Manuscript

By Kris Spisak

DAVRO PRESS

Copyright © 2020 by Kris Spisak

All rights reserved under the Pan-American and International Copyright Conventions. This book may not be reproduced, in whole or in part, in any form or by any means electronic or mechanical, including photocopying, recording, or by any information storage and retrieval system now known or hereafter invented, without written permission from the publisher, Davro Press.

The Novel Editing Workbook:
105 Tips & Tricks for Revising Your Fiction Manuscript

ISBN: 978-1-7344524-0-2

For further information on books from Davro Press, please visit DavroPress.com. For more information about Kris Spisak, her work, her speaking availability, and her books, please visit Kris-Spisak.com.

For the dreamers and the schemers, the plotters and the "pantsers," and anyone who has ever had a story inside them begging to come out. You are inspirations to us all, storytellers. Wherever you are in your process, keep going.

Acknowledgments

This book could never have been written without the storytellers who have fed my life—personally and professionally. From my early-childhood bedtime stories to the novels-in-progress that land on my editing desk these days, I have been gifted with tales true and imagined that have captivated me again and again. Thank you to my parents for getting that rolling and my clients who continue to impress me. I have to give a special shout-out, of course, to the many writing workshop attendees who purchased my first book, *Get a Grip on Your Grammar*, and then asked for more—you know who you are.

This project wouldn't be what it is without the assistance of Katharine Herndon, Lee Hawkins, Anne McAneny, and Leslie Saunderlin, and I am forever appreciative of Lisa Hagan, Karen A. Chase, Julie Valerie, and Frank Petroski for inspiring me, encouraging me, and partnering with me in so many ways. And finally, I have to note the James River Writers community. You all rock. It's that simple.

Aren't the possibilities of words and stories fascinating? If you agree, I'll thank you for your passion here too.

Contents

Why Edit?

ONCE UPON A TIME, A writer finished a manuscript. Cheering echoed in the air. Confetti blasted through the breeze. The people of the village lifted up the writer, carrying them atop shoulders, chanting a name that would be remembered in ink and in minds throughout the ages. Okay, perhaps this isn't quite how the story goes, but stay with me for a moment. This is how the story should go. Did you finish an entire novel? Huzzah, hooray, and props to you!

Are you done? Heck no, but take a moment to celebrate the glory of where you are. Do you know how many people have a dream of writing a novel? Do you know how many people actually do it?

You are in the minority, my friend, and if I could reach through the pages to give you a massive high five or an explosive fist bump, I would. Really. Boom.

Writers always wonder where to begin with their editing, but step one should always be a celebration. Whether it's a kazoo you blast out into an empty room (hopefully not a library and hopefully not while kids are asleep in a nearby bedroom) or whether it's a fist hammered into the air, take your moment. Be there. Thrive there. Take in the glory of your massive achievement.

Then take a deep breath. There's still lots of work ahead.

Once you get to your book's final page and type that last sentence's punctuation mark, you aren't really close to being finished. I know. Maybe the idea hurts, tired wordsmith, but let this truth sink in to your writer bones.

Editing is a stage of the writing process that must be embraced. It's your opportunity to tweak, cajole, twist your words like licorice, and buff the imperfections out of your sentences until they shine like new. It's your chance to transform that first draft that trickled out of your fingers and onto the page, turning your story into the book you want it to be.

If you're hoping to traditionally publish and think an agent or a publishing house's editor will do the heavy lifting, I'm sorry to say that it doesn't quite work that way. Your book must be as powerful as possible, cleaned up structurally, grammatically, and in so many other ways before any hope of a book deal.

If you're thinking of going the indie publishing route, "authorpreneurship" is indeed a more viable route than ever before, but this is a path you have to do right if you're looking for success. Heavy editing is essential here. A professional editor should indeed be a part of your indie publishing (aka "self-publishing") team, but all of that editing work is most profound and true to your story when it begins with you.

Whether you realize it or not, editing is energizing. It's the possibility of taking your solid creation and nudging it into the territory of brilliance. It's the possibility of taking a pile of words and shaping it into something that resembles the story you once envisioned. Sometimes, a book looks mighty ugly in its early draft form, but even rough, flawed words are so much better than a blank page. You've already conquered the blank page. No problem, right? Now it's time to push up your sleeves again, and with a little bit of direction, wow, can you get things done.

And you're ready to get that manuscript done, aren't you? All right, wordsmiths. Let's dive into strategies for novel-editing success.

How to Use This Workbook

IS EVERY EXERCISE IN this book something that you must do before you can call your book "finished"? No, not at all. Is every word choice question designed as a roadblock to your editing process? Hardly. Writers need assistance in different ways.

This workbook gives you fifty-three exercises and fifty-two questions to push your writing further (not farther) along on its journey. If you know where your weaknesses are, feel free to go straight into the appropriate section. That's why the Table of Contents is divided up as specifically as it is; however, I challenge you to think beyond what you know you need to do better. Often, the most powerful editing notes are the ones you've never previously considered.

If you're unsure, dabble. Do as many exercises as you can. The more you work on different aspects of your story, the stronger your work will be. If you begin any single exercise and realize it's not something that you need to work on, that's okay. Skip it. Move on. Just don't skip it because it's hard. Hard work is what makes things better. Hard work is what makes the difference between your soon-to-be-sparkling manuscript and so many others that are shared with the world still tarnished, untested, and so close yet oh so far away.

Writing a book is an intimidating idea, but you know what? You did it. Now finish the job.

So best of luck to you and your characters. Best of luck to the books you're working on now and the ones in your future. The editing process is essential to every novel that you write, but it gets easier the more you practice. I sincerely hope that this workbook enables you to think about your work, your words, and your novel in ways you may not have considered. You've got this, storytellers. Don't forget it for a second.

What is Editing?

"EDITING" INCLUDES ALL levels of revising your book, from the big-picture concept ideas to the tiniest punctuation mark details. Editing can be ensuring subject-verb agreement, but it can also be combining two characters into one. It can be the tightening of your sentences, getting rid of extraneous words, and it can be the reshaping of your manuscript, cutting scenes and chapters that don't fit with the whole. It can be seeking out that perfect verb or that perfectly captured setting.

The moment that final sentence is written, after the confetti settles in a writer's mind, it's wise to think of editing, but you have to be fully aware of what editing a novel means.

There are stages of editing that must occur, and they must occur in the right order.

There's the macro-edit—or big-picture edit—looking at your story in its entirety. Where does your story begin? Is this the best beginning? Does it work well with where you decide to end? Is your protagonist flat or easy to connect with? Are they an active player in your story or does the story "happen" to them? Is your antagonist cliché or multidimensional? Does your plotline meander aimlessly or do you have a focused narrative drive? Is your point of view consistent, and does it make the most sense for your story? Are your story elements (e.g., narration, dialogue, action) well balanced? There are so many big-picture questions to ask yourself, many of which require time and many of which require some heavy lifting to get right.

But please, folks. Don't skim for the perfect uses of "em dashes" versus "en dashes" versus hyphens (oh, there's a difference) before your story is as it should be.

The micro-edit, which focuses on sentence-level details, is a transformative piece of the process, but if you spend time with it too early, you might find yourself having to delete your brilliant changes altogether because of a later realization that a full scene has to be rewritten. Spending time on the perfect sentence needs to wait until your book's bones are perfectly in place.

Proofreading, as in the final editing stage, is the last sweep that seeks out any lingering imperfections—think grammar mistakes, punctuation flaws, and typos. If you're still changing a word here and there, you're still in the micro-edit phase. If you're on your final read-through, meticulously analyzing and approving every mark on the page, you're in the homestretch.

In short, begin at the beginning. Just know this doesn't mean sentence one of page one when it comes to revision. What do I mean? Read on to find out.

Pre-editing Necessities

Ready to jump in? Awesome. Let's start here: To be an effective editor of your own work, you need to have the right mind-set and the right preparations in place. Running forward full steam ahead, arms flailing through the air maniacally is perhaps something to applaud when it comes to your spirit; however, you can do better. You, writer, are a professional. You're an author. Authors know how to make this happen. (Flailing arms in the midst of an organized plan are, of course, acceptable. "Professional" doesn't mean that you can't have some fun along the way.)

So, before the primeval yell and your charge forward with red pen spears bravely poised in your grasp, let's talk pre-editing and what it really means.

Celebrate Yourself

A NONWRITER'S PERCEPTION of the writer's process sometimes slips into the back of our minds. You know what I'm talking about—the supportive friend who asks if you've "finished," the casual acquaintance who asks when your book comes out, the person who won't understand about that character in chapter two who has been bugging you for months because something's off with him, and you can't figure it out.

Celebrating yourself isn't always a natural impulse, but here's your step one. You, writer, are a rock star. You, writer, did it. You're not done, but your pages are filled to the brim with scribbles and stories and characters and translations from your brain into actual language that other people can understand. That, my friend, is awesome—and I mean "awesome" in the literal sense of the word. Writing is magic. Writing is capturing a little bit of that genius that you have hidden inside of you.

Don't turn the page until you're there. Seriously. This is important. There are so many highs and lows in the writer's life that we sometimes forget to celebrate our accomplishments along the way. It's self-care, but it's also a moment to appreciate what you can do when you set your mind on something.

· · · ·

EXERCISE #1: TOAST your water bottle (or your beverage of choice) to yourself. Buy yourself some chocolate or flowers or tacos. Run a victory lap around your neighborhood. Throw yourself a party. Invite your best writer or nonwriter friends, your family, your neighbors, or your pet hedgehog in an adorable party hat. Celebration is step one. It's essential. Don't move on until you've breathed it in, held your accomplishment in your lungs, and felt it trickle outward down your arms to your fingertips, down your belly and legs and ankles and toes. Only then should you continue.

Question #1:

Why shouldn't you talk about your "fictional novel"?

Take Time Away from Your Manuscript

YOU ARE MORE CONNECTED with your manuscript than anyone else could be. It is a part of you. You are a part of it. This is the brilliance of creativity, but it can also be a major hindrance to the editing process.

You know exactly what you want your novel to be, and when you are so close to a project, it's easy not to see it for what it actually is.

Time can make all the difference. We all have varying amounts of free time, of course, and we're all anxious about the next steps in our process. We want to move things along. I get it. However, giving yourself some time away from your project is essential. Yes, there's time involved in a book's creation—and no matter how long that was, you've conquered that piece, savvy writer!—yet there's also time needed to set your manuscript aside. Let it sit. And don't look at it. This is trickier than it sounds.

When you walk away from your novel, truly stay away from it. You'll be amazed at the new perspective you'll gain through this exercise. Separation makes the heart grow fonder, and separation makes editing eyes have a clarity that they wouldn't otherwise. You'll allow time for your story choices to settle in your mind. Maybe you'll feel good about them for the whole separation, but maybe something will keep niggling at you. Recognize those niggling feelings. They're signs there's something yet to be done. Just not yet.

· · · ·

EXERCISE #2: PUT DOWN your manuscript. Save the file, and do not open it or look at it for at least seven days. If you want a real challenge, make it thirty or sixty or ninety. Circle the date on your calendar that you're allowed to return to it, and use some willpower to hold strong. As long as you go back. Always go back.

Question #2:

If you want to build upon a new concept, do you want to "flesh out" or "flush out" your idea?

Become a Writer-Reader

ONE PIECE OF EDITING advice that so many people ignore is the fact that to be a great writer, you have to be a great reader. How are you expected to create powerful art if you never look at a painting, if you never look at the lines of a sculpture, if you never look at a paper-mâché mask that your art teacher showed you in elementary school before it was your turn to begin?

Writing is a craft. Becoming a more accomplished writer comes from practicing, but it also comes from being observant when you have words in front of you. Any words. These observations can come from reading novels like your own or reading books in a style brand-new to you. Poetry. Short stories. News articles. Plays. Screenplays. Audiobooks. Anything.

If you're reading and something's not working for you, ask yourself why. If you are drawn into a story, stop and ask yourself why. How did that author hook you? What is it about that character that makes you connect? What is it that draws the picture in your head so vividly that when you read you feel like you're watching a movie?

Now stop. How can you do that?

Being a good reader is just as important as anything else, if not more important than anything else. If you are serious about becoming a stronger writer, it's not a good idea to ignore all other writers for fear of emulating their style. Read everything. Read the great. Read the mediocre. Read outside your genre. Because only by reading will you have a comfort with words and an ease with language. Storytelling is an art. You've got to do your homework before becoming a master.

We all need readers in the world; however, as a writer, you need to be a reader too.

• • • •

EXERCISE #3: GO TO your bookshelf at home or go to your local library. Pull some books off the shelf. Read only their first pages. What is working? What pulls you in? What is successful? Jot down some notes. Read critically. Don't read to be immersed into the story. Instead read like a writer. What is it about the dialogue that intrigues you? Or the character? The setting? The pacing? The voice? The sentence structures? Take notes. Study. This is how you improve.

Question #3:

Is it time to "dive" in or "delve" in?

Maybe both could apply, but do you know
the difference?

Macro-Editing

IF YOU DIVE INTO THE fine-tooth combing of your manuscript, you'll be disappointed when your novel needs a massive haircut or hair extensions or some major untangling. The total story concept must work before any other editing comes into play. That means "macro-editing" or big-picture examinations of the whole to make sure everything is built as it should be.

Here's where you need to spend your time first. Let's talk about the big pieces, folks—your major story elements: structure, characters, plot, setting, and point of view.

First Page Essentials

SOME SAY A NOVEL NEEDS to start with a bang, and in some ways, this is a great idea. However, don't feel like this bang must be a gunshot or a dramatic, life-changing moment. Sometimes, the smallest of problems can have the most emotional pull if you present them in the right way. A single scene can hint at a larger plot. A single moment can introduce your protagonist in a way that connects your reader to them. There's a time and place for backstory and detail-packed descriptions, but your first page of your novel is not it. Set the mood. Set the scene. Set your character in your reader's mind. Then set things rolling.

• • • •

EXERCISE #4: LOOK AT the first page of your book and only the first page. Read it from the first sentence to the last sentence and stop. From reading only this, do you have an idea of the main character of your book? Do you have a hint of the problem that might be the main issue of the story? Does this first page fit in with the genre conventions of the project you're working on? (Remember Exercise #3 and the essential practice of reading extensively.) While addressing each of these questions is a challenge, it's something that needs to be done. This is entirely the point of the first page. Look at the first pages of favorite books for guidance, but after that, see where you are, determine where you need to go, and keep at it until you find the entrance point that makes the most sense for your story.

Question #4:

Is your character going through a "right" of passage, a "rite" of passage, or a "write" of passage?

This may or may not apply to your story, but knowing the right word is still worth it.

Final Page Essentials

EVERY SINGLE PROBLEM introduced through the course of your novel needs to addressed in some way by the final page. All issues don't need to be perfectly solved, but they all need to feel like they have come to a conclusion that will leave your reader satisfied. You're allowed to hint that there will be a next book in your series, if that's your goal, but you want to avoid making your reader feel like you forgot something.

There is also a certain symmetry that can exist—and often should exist—between your first page and your last page. A problem is introduced, and the problem is finally solved. A character enters the scene, and that character has evolved in some way. The first and last page should not only feel like they were written by the same writer, but they can also echo each other for a satisfying framing effect.

If the book starts with an apple plucked from a tree, perhaps it can end with an apple pie.

If the book starts with a crashing wave, perhaps it can end with calm waters.

There unfortunately is no rule for the perfect finish to your book. Endings take time and frequently many rewrites. But when you find that perfect ending, you'll know.

· · · ·

EXERCISE #5: READ THE last page of your book and ask yourself if it feels either rushed or incomplete somehow. You know that feeling when you finish a book and it seems like the author didn't quite stick the landing? As if they were on deadline and simply needed to wrap things up quickly? It's unsatisfying to a reader. As a writer, you know better.

Just because you are so excited to be done with this darn book doesn't mean you get to cheat. What detail has been left hanging? The solution doesn't always come easy, but if you think you're getting away with your ending, that lingering doubt is your red flag that you still have some work to do.

Conversely, if you're feeling unsatisfied with your ending, what would happen if you deleted your last sentence? What would happen if you deleted your last paragraph? Or the last page? When you write and rewrite that final chapter and that final page, spending so much time with it in this love-hate relationship, sometimes, you write straight past the perfect ending point. Sometimes the picture-perfect last sentence of a book is hiding in plain sight. Experiment. Imagine your book ending a few lines earlier. Or a few paragraphs earlier. Or even a few pages. Be brave in your experimentation. You never know what you'll find.

Question #5:

Are you trying to "shore up" or "sure up" your plot?

Chapter Start Essentials

JUST LIKE THE DECISION of where to start your book, the decision of where to start your chapter is something that's worth a second consideration. From time to time, the writing process requires some warm-up. Maybe the warm-up is stretching your fingers out over the keyboard, taking a couple deep breaths, or straightening your shoulders to better your posture while you're sitting at your desk. Other times, the warm-up is in the writing, but the problem is when this warm-up writing lingers in later manuscript drafts.

If your chapter begins as a character wakes up, as the sun rises, as they make their breakfast, as they get dressed, as your character walks through their neighborhood to get to the destination for the chapter, does this setup create the best possible start for what's about to happen? Writers sometimes need a warm-up, but your reader doesn't.

There is a big difference between writing-warm-up sections and the beginning of a chapter that is true and strong and powerful. A chapter start should pull a reader in immediately, continuing the story and keeping the reader closely connected with a character. If your chapter start is putting on slippers, pouring some orange juice, and brushing teeth, how captivating is this? Not captivating at all, right? You can do better.

• • • •

EXERCISE #6: EXAMINE the first paragraph of every chapter. Do you rehook your reader within that paragraph? If not, make it happen.

Question #6:

If you want to send a character's dog after a villain, would you "sic" the dog or "sick" the dog on them?

Chapter End Essentials

THE END OF A CHAPTER is the obvious place for your reader to stop reading. Maybe they're thinking about reaching for that bookmark. What can you do to stop them? What can you do to make them read on?

How can you make your reader curious about what's going to happen next? Or concerned for your protagonist? Or excited for the possibilities? How can you evoke the major problem—or plot—of the story to both stay on target and entice your reader with something more than just a satisfying closure to a scene?

Should the chapter end with a resolution of how your characters get off the cliff or with your character's knuckles turning white as their fingers are almost sliding off the edge? (Hey there, literal cliff-hanger.) Should the chapter end with the answer to a piece of the mystery or the revelation of the next clue? Should the chapter end with a sense of total satisfaction or a lingering doubt?

What can this look like with your story?

• • • •

EXERCISE #7: Read the final paragraph of every chapter. Are you inviting your reader to stop, or are you encouraging them to keep going? Always find a way to aim for the latter.

Question #7:

Is a villain planning on "extracting revenge" or "exacting revenge"?

Does Your Protagonist Have Agency?

I'M NOT TALKING ABOUT whether your character has a literary agency that could somehow represent you. Wouldn't that be a nice choose-your-own-adventure with a publishing deal twist?

We all want to be active players in our own life, right? Not someone pushed around by everything that happens to us. Characters are the same way. Reading a day-by-day accounting of someone is not as thrilling as reading a day-by-day, turn-by-turn, twist-by-twist story of a character taking charge of whatever situation they are in for better or worse, for guts and glory.

Do things happen to your character, or are they an active player in the story? Remember, a powerful protagonist should not only react to different circumstances. They need to make choices on their own. They need to have agency. They need to be an active player in their own story.

And remember, all of a character's choices and actions do not need to be the right choices and actions. Sometimes a choice fits a character's sense of self and their motivations, but this action is still something that can make your readers hold their breath. That terrible choice not only can redefine who they are as a character in a moment of struggle, but it may create a turning point in the plot of your story. Your reader might further connect to them as a flawed but relatable individual because of that terrible choice. We all try to be good people—at least, I like to think we do. However, if you write a perfect protagonist who is always doing the right thing, that's not a very exciting story to read.

• • • •

EXERCISE #8: FIND ALL of the moments in your story where the direction of the plot changes because of a character's choice. If you can't find any, you have some work to do.

Question #8:

Let's talk "heroine" vs. "heroin."
Which one is the drug, and which one is the female
lead of a story?

Are All of Your Characters Necessary?

CHARACTERS SHOULD BE complex. Every single one of yours needs to exist on your pages for a reason. They are more than passersby. They are the players on your stage. Too many can be confusing. Shared roles can be redundant. Each should be there with something to contribute, or else why did they wander into the spotlight at all?

Everything about your book needs to be there for a reason. Your characters are no different.

• • • •

EXERCISE #9: LIST EVERY character named in your book. Do you have any characters who share similar roles, who might be more effective as one combined character instead of multiple? Do any characters appear for such a short time in your story that they might not need a name at all and could simply be "the bank teller," "the waitress," "the window washer," or a similarly unnamed yet acknowledged individual? (Why give your readers something to latch onto when it's a character who is about to walk away for good?)

Question #9:

What is the plural of "passerby"?

Create Unique Characters

DO YOU KNOW WHAT'S awesome about people? We are all different. We see the world differently. We act differently. We look different. We come in all shapes, shades, and sizes. So if your characters behave like one another—with the same mannerisms, with the same expressions on their faces—it doesn't seem real. This is first-draft writing sometimes, sure, but first-draft writing can always be improved.

The publishing world is competitive. There are more writers writing than ever. This is awesome, isn't it? But it also means you need to up your game.

Get to know your characters. Maybe one of them always finds that pebble to kick while he walks down the street. Maybe one picks at his fingernails. Maybe one absentmindedly braids the loose strands of the yarn bracelet she always wears. Maybe one constantly pulls at the collar of their shirt. Maybe one always positions herself where she can see all the entrances to the room.

Should every character kick a pebble when walking down the street? No, that would be strange. Every person doesn't have the same habits. Every person doesn't have the same mannerisms. If you asked ten people to sit around a table, none of them would sit and be still in the same way.

Give each character the opportunity to be distinctive. Only then will they be alive to your readers—and having characters who are alive to your readers is not only what makes readers keep reading but also what makes them want to pick up your next book.

• • • •

EXERCISE #10: LOOK at the people around you. Study the way they are still. Study the way they move. Highlighting these mannerisms and subconscious actions amidst your dialogue and the bigger moments of your plot is a way of letting your reader know your characters better. It allows them to be vivid on the page amidst your greater story.

Question #10:

Do you have a character who might "nash," "knash," or "gnash" his or her teeth? Wait, how do you spell that word again?

(Or is it the editing process making you do that? I sure hope not!)

Give Your Characters Emotional Tells

HOW YOU SHOW NERVOUSNESS or eagerness or anger or sadness or giddiness is unique to you. Your family and friends can probably tell when you're annoyed without you saying a word. They can probably tell when you're frustrated and when you're thrilled. How? Because they can read you.

Know your characters so well that you can give your readers similar clues. Allow them to not only read about your characters. Allow them to truly "read" each and every one of them and the clues they share without ever meaning to.

Readers love following clues. Emotional clues are no different. "Showing vs. telling" is a conversation we can weave into many aspects of your writing, but when it comes to feelings, here's your opportunity to make your characters come alive.

• • • •

EXERCISE #11: MAKE a list of all of your characters. Think about how they physically respond to different emotions. You can do this in a spreadsheet with characters listed along the x-axis and emotions listed along the y-axis, taking the time to fill in every blank. You can do this in a freewriting brainstorm if spreadsheets aren't your style. Then bring these specifics into your pages.

Question #11:

Is your character not "phased" by another's action or not "fazed" by it?

Is There a Focused Plot & Narrative Drive?

DOES YOUR BOOK HAVE a problem that drives the story forward, or are we following a character going about their day? Is there a cohesive concern at the core of the story that drives every moment?

Sometimes first drafts are made up of collections of happenings that—brilliant as they may be—are a bit disconnected. One story tangent after another does not make a novel. A reader can follow a character through their day, but when reading your book, they should follow a character along the path of a story, also known as the plot.

There needs to be a major problem, a focus, a drive, a carrot on a stick, a quest, a dream, a goal, and/or a fear that terrifies them. A novel, no matter the story, needs to be a journey that carries a reader from page one until the final scene. It cannot simply follow a character as they wake up and things happen. It cannot be the wittiest of witty dialogue alone—or the funniest of circumstances or the most fascinating of situations or the most profound of moments.

Every chapter and every scene must be related to the plot in some way.

Maybe a scene brings hardships for your protagonist; maybe a scene is a moment of hope; maybe your characters are getting close to their goal or being pushed further away from it. Every single scene must be related in some way, and if it is not, does it deserve to be a part of your book?

This brings up that famous quote of "kill your darlings" (thanks for that one, William Faulkner).

Sometimes our best sentences or most poignant scenes or most fascinating backstories are off topic. In the editing phase, this is where you dive deep and figure out where you are going and if you're going there effectively. A powerful book doesn't stray from its plot, or if it does seem to stray, it strays with thoughtful author intention.

• • • •

EXERCISE #12: DO A post-first-draft outline of your novel. This can take any form you'd like, from bullet points in a new document to index cards on a bulletin board to your favorite writing software app. Jot down a sentence or two about what happens in every scene. Now check every scene against the plot or problem of your book. Do you find anything that's not related? If so, it's time to start debating those scissors. Be willing to take a look at every moment in your book critically. Then be honest with yourself with what you find and what needs to be done about it.

Yes, some books have more than one plotline. If this is the case for you, you may double-check your scenes against your two plots (or however many you have). The more complicated your book, the more complicated this exercise, but it applies all the same.

Question #12:

If a character is in a stage of difficulty, are they "in the throws" of something or "in the throes" of it?

Are All of Your Scenes Necessary?

PLOTTERS, THIS SHOULD be easy. Pantsers ... well ... hold on to your pants.

(And by "pantsers," I mean writers who do not outline and who write "by the seat of their pants," of course.)

If a scene isn't moving your plot forward, further establishing a character, or enhancing a reader's understanding of the larger issues at play in your book, it might be a tangent from your story. Tangents, I'm sorry to say, are something for the chopping block. Every chapter, every paragraph, every page, every sentence, and every word in your book must serve the greater purpose.

Beyond reaffirming that every scene is related to your book's plot, as we've discussed previously, double-check that each scene adds something to the whole. Be honest with yourself as you assess the purpose and rationale behind every scene. And if it has no purpose or rationale, that's telling you something. Watch out for duplicate moments, dwelling-over-what's-happened-so-far moments, or anything that doesn't further raise the stakes or give your reader something new to chew on.

· · · ·

EXERCISE #13: RETURN to that post-first-draft outline of your novel, which you've probably already created from Exercise #12. Not only must each scene be related to your plot, but it also needs to move the story forward in some way. If there's no change or further understanding at the end of the scene (i.e., change in the circumstances or change in the character), why is it there? Beware of thinking scenes especially. Your reader doesn't need as much review as you might think.

Question #13:

If your character is trying to figure something out, are they "pouring" over their research books or "poring" over them?

Reassess Your Sitting & Talking Scenes

WHEN IT COMES TO BOOK editing, it's best to remember that actions—big or small—can be more powerful than superfluous dialogue. Dialogue can sometimes be the best part of a book, but the story needs to lead the way, not the characters repetitively talking it out.

Discovering things about yourself, your world, the meaning of life, or the meaning of the clue that answers the murder mystery all within a conversation might be a life-changing for a person but not always for a reader. Readers are pulled into stories. Wait, let me clarify that. Readers are pulled into stories when they are transported into a moment with your character, experiencing the same hopes, fears, anticipation, and every other emotion by that character's side.

Brilliant dialogue is something to celebrate, but remember your job as a novelist is to craft more than only brilliant dialogue, especially when that dialogue is not surrounded by anything that actually happens. If you're writing a novel, you can't forget the character's story, the problem driving the plot, and the internal and external forces at play. Sometimes sitting-and-talking scenes—in a car, at a diner, on a park bench, leaning on a pillow, or anywhere else—are either talking for the sake of talking or talking for such a duration that the story's plot and its urgency are lost. That's a big red flag. You can't lose your story. What else are you writing but a story?

Actions speak louder than words. It's true for your characters as much as yourself.

• • • •

EXERCISE #14: SEEK and destroy sitting-and-talking scenes. Just kidding. Well, I'm only kind of kidding. They should only exist rarely and only make the final cut if something is accomplished in that conversation more than a review of happenings or a Socratic dialogue.

Question #14:

If you have a character who is trying their best to be patient, are they waiting with "baited breath" or "bated breath"?

Are Any Scenes Missing or Rushed?

THERE'S A QUICK SUMMARY of a moment, and then there's writing that allows your readers to live through a scene, standing shoulder to shoulder with your characters.

Pull your reader in. Don't forget the sights, the sounds, the smells, the movements big or small by those all around, and the specifics of the surroundings. Do you give the most important moments in your novel enough time and space to have the effect you want? Or are they rushed?

Some scenes can be short and haunting. There's nothing wrong with a "fade to black" if a "fade to black" is what your novel needs. However, don't skip over something that your readers will feel slighted about if you rush. Does your entire book suffer because of the absence of a critical scene that started the entire plot moving but that isn't exposed on your pages? Will your reader feel cheated when that big thing—that big thing they've been waiting for with bated breath—happens, but they don't get to live through it with your characters? Is there a pivotal moment for your story that you include but don't spend as much time with as you should?

There's a fine line, of course, between fleshing out a scene and having so much text that you need to tighten and pull back in the other direction, but both sides of this equation need to be examined before you can call your story done.

• • • •

EXERCISE #15: AT THE end of every chapter, pause and consider the scenes that made up that chapter. Consider whether any of them were rushed or if you gave your readers an opportunity to sink their teeth into each moment with your character(s)?

Question #15:

If you, as the writer, missed something that you now realize you should return to, would you say you "passed up the opportunity" or "past up the opportunity" to fully tackle that moment in your earlier drafts?

(The answer to this question is coming soon, but at least you can go back to your manuscript and edit away!)

Does the Setting Come Through?

COULD YOUR STORY HAPPEN anywhere? In the prewriting stage of your manuscript, maybe you spent a long time with your setting, when and where your novel takes place. Maybe you did a deep dive, considering all of your senses, thinking about how the locations of your book look, smell, sound, or feel. These are valuable details to explore. However, they're also valuable details to return to in the editing phase, because often the best of intentions can be forgotten.

You need to make sure you're not accidentally being lazy about your sense of place amidst the action, amidst your characterization, and amidst your dialogue. Adding a single beat, even a single sentence of atmosphere and place, can go far in bringing a scene from a blank movie screen to something profound in your reader's imagination.

• • • •

EXERCISE #16: GO BACK to your manuscript and think of all of the major settings that you have—a park, a bar, a planet hidden in the vertical rings of Neptune. Wherever your locations, make sure they are real for your readers.

Make a list of ten specific details about each one of these settings. Don't tell your readers there is a room with tables; tell them about the refurbished barn doors used as tabletops. Don't mention there's wallpaper; write about how that wallpaper is stained red in the corner and how that red may or may not be blood. After you list ten details for each place, return to your scenes. Where are your opportunities to make them vivid for your readers?

Do you need to insert all ten details? Of course not. But these places need to be alive in your mind before you can transport your reader there.

Question #16:

If you mention the details of a character's apartment that showcase how it's decorated to suit their personality, would you talk about the "flair" of the space or "flare" of it?

P.O.V. Consistency

HEY THERE, WRITER. This is me talking to you. This is a second-person voice, like in a love letter. (Yep, I'm getting kind of attached to you at this point). Second-person is rare but not unheard of in a novel. There's also a first-person point of view, writing in the voice of one of your characters (e.g., I, me, we...), and then there's third-person, where your narrator isn't a part of the story (referencing characters with "he," "she," "they," etc.).

Decisions about point of view are important, as is being consistent with this choice.

Sometimes the point of view of a story comes into an author's head before they ever write the first word. Maybe it's a conscious decision. Maybe it's something you've waffled on and experimented with. Just remember, in the end, that you've got to stick with your point of view choice. One sentence out of one chapter haphazardly taking a step away from this format is jarring.

If you choose to write in third person, of course, that is not the end of your choice. Consider whether you're writing in "third-person omniscient," which means that you as a narrator are allowed to be inside of the head of every character that enters your pages, knowing their thoughts, motivations, dreams, hopes, and fears. Or, perhaps, you're writing in "third-person limited," only able to enter into the thoughts of your protagonist with all other characters slightly more distanced. Writing in "third-person objective" would mean that you never know the internal thoughts of any of your characters except for what is exposed on your pages by the narrator's outside observations.

Point of view (lovingly referred to as "p.o.v.") is a complicated matter, and if you're new to these ideas, it's worth some further study. But for editing purposes, know that it's essential that you understand your chosen p.o.v. and stick with it consistently. Yes, it's true that you can write a novel with multiple points of view, but if you choose to do so, recognize that your challenge is even more difficult.

• • • •

EXERCISE #17: WRITE down your story's point of view. Write it on the sidebar of your title page. Write down the rules of this p.o.v. as you understand them. What does your narrator know? Whose heads are they allowed into, in regards to knowing hopes and dreams and fears and motivations? Only one character's? Many characters'? What would your narrator know beyond the scope of a single scene?

Be aware of the possibilities and limitations of your point of view choice. Anything is possible, but so much more is possible if you handle your work well. Do not stray from the p.o.v. choices you've made for your book. Use your written notes on your sidebar as your guide for your full project. Reference these notes regularly if you're ever concerned you're off the mark.

Question #17:

This editing process takes time, but sometimes you have to "grin and bear it." Or is it "grin and bare" it?

Set Your Editing Course

WHEN YOU'RE GETTING ready to run a marathon, you can't think about the entire marathon. You think about the steps immediately ahead. And first things first, you need to know your path.

One way to begin is by doing some prep work. I know you're probably itching to set out on page one, line one, with your red pen (metaphorical or literal) poised at the ready, but diving in while thinking about conquering the whole project will exhaust you before you've gotten very far at all.

You need to create the road signs that will remind you what that path is when it's racing time and you're on the move. Every project, no matter what it is, is better with a plan of action in place.

• • • •

EXERCISE #18: COLLECT some symbols that you know are nowhere in your manuscript. Think about asterisks (*), carets (^), plus signs (+), a tilde (~), or maybe a triple pound (###). Assign each of these symbols to something you're working on. Pull these ideas from the macro-editing focuses in the previous section or pull them from your own to-do list.

For example:

- *^ - weak setting/atmosphere*
- *+ - missing emotional intensity*
- *~ - weak transition*
- ** - scene that's rushed*
- *### - more research needed here*

Imagine yourself as a race organizer setting the course, and read through your completed manuscript. The challenge is to not make a single editorial change upon your pages, only the road signs for the effort ahead. Yes, this is easier said than done.

Why did I say to use symbols that aren't already in your manuscript? Because this makes them searchable. By using the "Find" function, a tool that we're going to return to again and again in the micro-editing process (stay tuned for more details), you can now seek out every spot where your character is passive in their own story, where your action needs more effort, where your dialogue runs on without support from any other story elements, or whatever it is you decide is important. The editing task that each symbol is assigned to is totally up to you. (And yes, many more ideas for these are ahead).

The important part of this exercise is only the course-setting, though. Make your marks but not any changes yet. Ready, set, go!

Question #18:

If you're working on an updated version of a previously published book, is it a second "addition" or a second "edition"?

Edit in Waves

HAVING A PLAN IS INSTRUMENTAL. But having that plan, should you tackle steps one through thirty-three at the same time? Of course not. That would be silly. Yet, do you know what we do again and again as writers? We start editing on page one, sentence by sentence, because that is how we're convinced we need to slog through revisions.

Hold your horses, folks, and with those horses, of course, hold all of those clichés that have slipped into your writing. We'll take care of those later.

By editing in waves, conquering one aspect of your revision at a time, you allow yourself to home in on what's not working and to focus on improvements. Your brain and your fingertips on the keyboard have time to practice and problem solve. If you don't edit in waves and simply jump from one area that needs a fix to the next—with each problem unique—you won't be able to get into nearly the same groove.

Plus, how sweet does it feel to strike one completed item off your editing to-do list? If you're going page by page with your revisions, it will take you an awfully long time before you can cross anything off your list. Editing in waves is both effective and empowering. And who wants anything but effective and empowering editing? (I'm guessing you're not raising your hand.)

• • • •

EXERCISE #19: IF YOU'VE created your roadmap (see Exercise #18), start in with one piece of it at a time. Search your manuscript for any one of the symbols you used as markers. Focus in on only that one piece of your editing, and jump from tilde to tilde to tilde until you have worked through every weakness in a particular area. Then move on to the next. Jump from caret to caret, then asterisk to asterisk.

Question #19:

Does this editing process make you want to "hunker down" or "bunker down"? Or at least answer this: what's the correct version of this phrase?

Embrace To-Do Lists

WHETHER YOU PUT YOUR editing to-do list into a spreadsheet like Microsoft Excel or Google Sheets, into a document, or on some sticky notes hanging up on your wall doesn't matter. We all have our ways. Maybe yours involves index cards on a poster board or list-making apps in the Cloud.

And yes, the best part of lists is striking items off when you're finished. Bold black permanent markers are awesome for this. Tearing sticky notes off a bulletin board is a similarly satisfying experience (though watch out for flying tacks). There's always a jab of a finger on a digital checklist too (perhaps not quite as satisfying, but to each their own).

Organization is essential for editing. Celebrating your baby steps as you check off your to-do list tasks should be too. Make a plan, and you can change the world. Maybe that change right now simply involves your latest manuscript.

* * * *

EXERCISE #20: PLAY with three different to-do list formats. Jot down your tasks at your computer, on a notepad on your desk, on a smartphone, or any way you can think to do it. But make yourself start this list in three different ways. What's most important to you about a to-do list? Having it with you wherever you go? Being able to see it all at a glance? The feeling of striking an item off by physically drawing a line through it? The ability to easily prioritize and rearrange the order? The capability to meticulously categorize and organize the details?

By forcing yourself to attempt this list-making in three different ways, you'll most likely find that one feels most comfortable to you. And finding that organizational strategy sooner rather than later is a good thing. Once you've figured it out, start breaking down what you know you need to do to enhance your book. (If you're short on ideas, don't worry at all. Many more are coming your way in the following pages.)

Question #20:

Is that project you're working on a
"work-in-progress" or a "work-in-process"?

("#wip" won't help you with this one.)

Micro-Editing

IF YOU FLIPPED AHEAD and are starting your editing journey, this is where I'm going to ask you to freeze and take twenty giant steps back.

"Mother, may I?" you ask.

Yes, you absolutely may.

In fact, I wouldn't have it any other way. Writers—myself included—really want to dig into that final sweep. They want to call the project they've loved and hated and slaved over "complete." I get it. I'm with you. But think about how much time you've put into your work-in-progress. Do you want the final product to be less than what it could be because you got antsy at the end?

Deep breath, writers. You've got this.

When you're ready for micro-editing—and by "micro-editing," I mean the detail-oriented, line-by-line examination of your book to ensure every paragraph, sentence, and word is what it should be—you're approaching that finish line. Maybe you've gotten your second wind. Maybe you're crawling along. But you're so close. Keep going!

And when you're ready ... let's do this thing!

Question #21:

Button down the hatches, writers. Things are about to get intense! Or should you "batten" them down?

Amplifying Your Word Choice

Discover the Power of Verbs

THE KEY TO MICRO-EDITING is remembering that even though you used a word in the creation of your novel's first draft, this doesn't mean that it's the word you should use forever. Verbs are a great place to begin this conversation.

You need to have your verbs correct, of course—not swapping out a "lay" for a "lie" or an "insure" for an "ensure"—but beyond correctness, verbs are your opportunities to bring your writing from blah to brilliant. Sometimes, the first verb you thought of in your rough draft will do, but other times, this less-than-perfect choice makes your writing sound like something a reader has read countless times before.

I have three verb considerations for you (ooh, look! Bonus editing tips!):

First, verbs should do more than just "be." Rethink your usages of the verb "to be." He was. She was. They were. It is. There are. Are you weakening your writing by using the verb "to be" too much? Could your writing be more vivid with a different verb choice, perhaps allowing your sentences to be more active and original?

Second, if your verb relies on an adverb, think of the better word choice. A character can "tiptoe" rather than "walk softly." She can "bolt" rather than "run fast." He can "scrub" rather than "wipe vigorously."

Third, think beyond the first word that comes to your mind. Read your work like a detective looking for weak links. Sometimes verb choices are adequate, but seize upon opportunities to be better.

We don't all need to be poets, but we do need to take the time to reconsider our language. Amp up and revitalize your prose. Cultivate your originality. Intensify your language. Coax out your possibilities.

• • • •

EXERCISE #21: SEARCH for "was," "were," "is," and "are" in your pages. In many cases, these words are a reasonable word choice, but look for openings where you can write a more powerful line. Maybe a sentence can become more active. Maybe it can have a stronger subject. Maybe it can be flipped on its head.

• • • •

EXERCISE #22: SEARCH for "ly" within your manuscript. (Here's that lovely "Find" function coming into play.) Will this catch every adverb? No. But chances are it will be enough to make this exercise worthwhile. Look for adverbs that modify verbs, where you can come up with a stronger word choice. Challenge yourself as a writer to find the perfect word, not the almost perfect combination.

• • • •

EXERCISE #23: READ your sentences closely, paying attention to every verb. Where are the verbs that you overuse? We all have them. Try to find yours. Seek them out and rewrite sentences as needed so your reader isn't distracted by repetitive actions. (We'll get to some of these in the following pages.)

Question #22:

Did your character's grandmother "instill" values or "install" values in your character?

The "It Was" Challenge

OKAY, OKAY, I HEAR you. "It was the best of times. It was the worst of times." Yes, this is one of the most well-known openings in literature, but just because a book is a classic doesn't mean it couldn't have used some better editing.

> "It was a sunny day outside."
> "It was a crowd of people, pitchforks in hand."
> "It was the best bourbon she ever had."

"It was" is simply a lazy sentence start. (And bonus tip: "there are" and "there is" aren't that far behind.)   What does that "it" even mean when it's used as a sentence subject like this? Please tell me. I'll wait ... waiting ... waiting ... you don't know, do you? And if you don't even know what the antecedent of a pro-noun is, should you use it?

There's nothing incorrect with "It was" sentences. On occasion, they can remain in your manuscript because perhaps they are indeed the best fit; however, these are the sentences that are made for reexamination. Often, they're made for revision. They are golden opportunities waiting to be discovered and transformed into something much more brilliant. Or if not brilliant, at least more comprehensible or more focused.

> "The sun didn't have a single cloud to hide behind."
> "A crowd of people, pitchforks in hand, chanted his name again and again."
> "She took a sip of the best bourbon she ever had."

You might catch these "It was" sentences when you do your verb elevation work from Exercise #21, but the "It was" challenge deserves a moment in the spotlight here too.

• • • •

EXERCISE #24: SEARCH for "It was" in your manuscript. Use every one you find as an opportunity to rethink the sentence. An "it was" sentence is rarely the best that you can do.

• • • •

EXERCISE #25: SEARCH for "there is," "there are," "there was," and "there were" as well. Vague sentence starts can take away the power of your prose. Don't let them.

Question #23:

Should I say, "Every once and a while," you might be able to get away with these wordings, or should I say, "Every once in a while," you could do it?

The Tiresome Sentence Structure Challenge

SOMETIMES, WE FALL into a writing rut without even realizing it. Our sentence structure is one of the first pieces that falls victim to lazy writing.

Tell me if a paragraph like this might sound familiar:

"He grabbed the tickets out of her hand. He glanced away when she looked up at him. He dug his toe into the dust of the street. He loved her. He wasn't going to lose her like this."

Do you see the problem? He ... he ... he ... Nothing against the guy, but he's not helping the writer here.

Now, notice the difference when the lazy example is updated:

"He grabbed the tickets out of her hand. When she looked up at him, he glanced away, digging his toe into the dust of the street. He loved her. Losing her like this wasn't an option."

Suddenly, the flow is easy and smooth. (And yes, I wrote "suddenly," a word I don't use frequently, as you'll soon know from Exercise #31). Taking the time to smooth out your writing can make all the difference.

• • • •

EXERCISE #26: TURN to page 113 of your manuscript. Pick the longest paragraph there and analyze your sentence beginnings. Is there repetition? No? Awe-some. Yes? Maybe you still have some work to do on this note.

The true exercise would be to do a sentence subject editing wave through your entire manuscript. I highly suggest it in fact. Usually, somewhere after page 75, writers tend to get lethargic. All the work and effort they've put in starts getting *tiresome, and strange things happen. Sometimes, these strange things lead to char-acters with swapped names or accidental shifts in point of view. Sometimes, it's a matter of lazy sentence structure. At least that's a fixable problem. Fixable prob-lems are a good thing.*

Question #24:

If you're bringing your reader into a past time period, are you writing "historic" or "historical" fiction?

Think on Your Ten-Dollar Words

SHOWING OFF YOUR VOCABULARY chops can be absolutely awesome. When there is the absolute right word for a situation and when you find it perfectly placed, it's a little bit of magic, isn't it? You know what I'm talking about.

However, trying to push an erudite vocabulary is another matter. What you are writing and who you are writing for are the questions to consider here. Your goal is to craft your language in a way that your reader understands. Do you ever use vocabulary that will trip them up too frequently? I am all about the right word for the right situation—whatever that language might be—but be sure you don't lose your reader in the process of using it.

If your language is distracting because you're using ten-dollar words too frequently, your readers might not appreciate what you're doing. Am I saying to dumb down your work? Absolutely not, but be thoughtful about your target audience and where they are as they're coming to your book.

Be especially thoughtful in the repetition of unique vocabulary words. If you're able to drop in one of those magic words that makes a sentence shine, that's awesome. But if you then use that outstanding word on the next page, that word that once caught your reader's attention for its perfection will start to sound tiresome. Tiresome is absolutely something to avoid.

• • • •

EXERCISE #27: YOU KNOW that collection of words you're so super proud of in your book? I know you know them, the ones you tucked in so perfectly that your chin raised slightly higher? Go back to those words and make sure you're using them well. Or if your everyday vocabulary is more elevated than the average reader, consider your advanced language. Find a way to be intelligent yet still accessible.

Question #25:

Your editing work should run the gamut from big-picture revision to proofreading for the tiniest of details. Or should it "run the gambit"? Or should it "run the gauntlet"?

Enabling Your Reader to Experience Your Story

Don't Name Emotions. Evoke Them.

WE'VE TALKED ABOUT how you can use "emotional tells" to give clues to your readers about your characters' feelings (see Exercise #11). We've talked about these unique mannerisms as distinguishing traits that allow your readers to further connect with your characters (see Exercise #10). Yet this is a micro-editing note you need to spend some time with too.

If in one scene, your character is terrified, what is more powerful?

"Topher is terrified."

or

"Topher tightened his fists and fought the urge to vomit."

What kind of writer do you want to be? Do you want to summarize, or do you want to bring your reader into a moment?

. . . .

EXERCISE #28: SEARCH the name of every emotion word you can think of in your manuscript. Seek out "happy," "mad," "excited," "worried," "nervous," "sad," and more. If you find these words, they are chances to rewrite and add more "showing" and less "telling." Don't name the emotion. Evoke it with your characters' actions so your reader understands. It's an easy way to bring your writing to the next level.

Question #26:

Should a character have a nervous "tick"
or a nervous "tic"?

Review the Scaling of Emotions

EMOTIONS ARE REAL, and every one of us could be set off in one way or another with the correct prompt. Is this my exercise? No, let's not go there. But you should be careful with characters who go from happy-go-lucky to irate within the beat of a single sentence.

Sometimes writers forget that emotional build is necessary. Disturbed to irritated to exasperated to being at our wit's end doesn't happen in a single flare in most situations. Of course, maybe you do have that character with a temper, and maybe this note does not apply to him. Yet, I'm going to have you think about him in this regard too.

Imagine watching an angry character slowly become calmer then pacified then intrigued by something then excited about it. That emotional variance within a single scene can pull a reader in if you take the time to do it well. If you don't, it becomes jumpy, and your characters become a little manic—and I'm guessing that's not what you're going for.

• • • •

EXERCISE #29: EVERY time your characters have a shift in emotions during the scene, reexamine how you do it. Is it too fast? Do you allow your readers time to go on the emotional journey with your characters? Allow them to see and experience the subtleties that trigger the changes. It's all about bringing them along for the ride.

Question #27:

Should you write about a hungover character waking up feeling "grisly" or "grizzly"?

Strike the Realizations

THERE ARE A NUMBER of words that are examples of where a writer is cheating. Do I mean cheating where whistles are blown and flags are tossed onto the field? No. Though, if I had my way, it might be something like that. I mean "cheating" because the writer is taking the easy way out, and their writing suffers for it.

Your goal as a writer is to invite your readers into your characters' journey—into their lives, making every discovery by their side. When it comes to the word "realize," would you rather have your reader hear about what is being discovered, or would you rather have your reader make the discovery along with your characters? What is more exciting?

What is more powerful: a line about a character realizing the solution to the mystery or a moment that allows your reader to have the same epiphany as your protagonist at the same time? What will strike your reader more profoundly: an injustice experienced through a scene or the pointing out that something is not fair? What might draw your reader in more: the witnessing of the exact second she understands she loves him or the narration where this revelation is explained to the reader?

It's harder. It takes more time. But when it comes to doing things well, aren't you up to that challenge?

• • • •

EXERCISE #30: YOUR opportunity here is to search out the word "realize" in your manuscript—and when I say search out the word "realize," I actually mean to search out "realiz" because if you stop at the "z," you will catch the words "realize," "realized," "realizing," and every other version that might pop up. Of course, "realize" is not the only epiphany-weakening culprit. Think about other wordings you use in the same way too. Then take these opportunities to elevate the possibilities. Your reader will appreciate it.

Question #28:

Your character might just have realized their plan isn't working. Should they "change tact" or "change tack"?

The "Suddenly" Challenge

THE WORD "SUDDENLY," at its core, does not make any moment more exciting than it is otherwise. Think about it.

> "He jumped out from behind the wall suddenly."
> "Suddenly, she screamed."
> "Suddenly, the shadow grew into a monster that loomed over the height of the surrounding buildings."

Yes, this word seems great for adding momentum and intensifying your pacing and suspense; however, "suddenly" is a word that is abused and overused. Sometimes "suddenly" is a red flag that you are not editing hard enough.

When "suddenly" is sprinkled like a springtime shower all over your action scenes, your text ends up soggy. You can get away with first-draft wordings in first drafts, but later on, it's time to push yourself and keep up the great work you've already started. There's no "suddenly" in the editing process unfortunately—these things take time. However, upping your game is one way to empower the journey.

• • • •

EXERCISE #31: USE THE "Find" function to discover how many times you use "suddenly" in your manuscript. If it's not many, you're probably fine. If it's a lot, it's time to get back to work. Create the suspense without this word that sneaks in so frequently when it thinks no one's looking (oh, but readers are always looking).

Question #29:

Think fast: Is it "all of the sudden" or "all of a sudden"?

Challenge Your First-Draft Sentence Lengths

SHORTER SENTENCES REPEATED one after another help with writing action. Your reader wants to move faster, and the shorter sentences let them. Imagine a sword fight. There's a jab. A stab. A slice of the sword through the air. Put these actions into short, staccato sentences, and you've discovered a secret of writing suspense. Weird but true.

Conversely, longer sentences slow down a moment. They can allow your reader a reprieve after a suspenseful scene. When thoughtfully composed, they can pull a reader into the details of a moment or a place.

We all have patterns that we fall into when it comes to the lengths of our sentences. Some of us love long, wending, meandering sentences. Some of us would rather get to the point: subject, verb, done. Whatever your preferred structure might be, you have to make sure that you are not falling into a rhythm that becomes tiresome or difficult to read for whoever has your book open. You have to ensure your sentence length matches what you are trying to achieve in any given paragraph.

We fall into ruts with our writing. Reexamining the length of our sentences can be valuable because it's where you allow your best writer self to show up. And your best writer self should always show up, if not in the drafting, at least in the editing phase.

• • • •

EXERCISE #32: GO TO page 103 of your finished manuscript. Have I seen your finished manuscript? Of course not, but bear with me for this exercise. If for some reason you do not have a page 103, open up your file and pick a page in the middle.

On this page, pick a single paragraph, ideally the longest one on the page. Now write that exact paragraph again using sentences that are as short as possible (e.g., "He ran. She jumped. They saw."). Whatever your sentences happen to be, make it happen—no matter if it's dialogue, exposition, action, or otherwise. Then, once you've done that, try again, but this time see how long you can possibly make those sentences. Can you craft them to be stretched out and slow, going on for miles? Maybe this is where you pull out those lovely semicolons; perhaps we all could use some practice with the proper use of semicolons beyond winky faces anyway.

When you're finished, read your short-sentence version. Read your long-sentence version. Rewrite it a third time however you'd like. Maybe all you're going to do is bring it back to exactly the form where it was in the beginning, yet maybe, through this exercise, you've seen where some sentences work well short, while others work well long. It's time to discover the power of mixing your sentence length to embolden the whole.

Question #30:

Do you know the difference between being "uninterested" and "disinterested"?

Some might be uninterested in all of these craft subtleties, but you, storyteller, are officially bringing your A game.

Reconsidering Character Actions

Think Beyond the Eyes

FIRST DRAFTS OF MANUSCRIPTS are often obsessed with eyes. You might not even realize it's the case, but chances are you have overwritten eyes in your writer life.

Do your characters stare, glare, look, glance, lock eyes, meet eyes, shift their eyes, narrow their eyes and/or squint? There is nothing wrong with any of these actions or any reference to the eyes, but when all of your character movement, body language, and narration between dialogue is focused on the eyes and only the eyes, not only is it repetitive, but you are missing opportunities for characters to come alive.

People are so much more than their eyes and what their eyes look at. You can do so much better. Don't miss your best opportunities for storytelling elevation.

• • • •

EXERCISE #33: SEARCH your manuscript for "look," "stare," "eye," and other words related to these. Examine each and every usage and how frequently you use these eye references. Do you dare to give yourself the challenge of striking the majority of them and coming up with other ways to express character interactions and small movements? This is an exercise that can be eye-opening, pun absolutely intended.

Question #31:

Does your protagonist do too much "naval-gazing"? Or is it "navel-gazing"?

Clean up Mechanical Movements

IF A CHARACTER PUTS their right arm in and then their right arm out and then their left hip in and then their left hip out, they are either doing the hokey pokey or you're getting too granular in your descriptions of movements.

Specificity in your descriptions pulls readers in and activates their imaginations. You could write about "a man on the corner of the street," or you could write about "the stranger who drummed his fingers on the black metal of the last mailbox on the street." You could write about "the cat curled up in the chair," or you could write about "the tuxedo kitten whose tail curved around its body to cover up its nose."

Yet there's another side of this to consider. In your specificity, do not work so hard that you end up sounding like an instruction manual. There is no need to specify that he lifted his right hand to a forty-five-degree angle to block out the sun that was shining at a three o'clock position in the afternoon sky.

The goal is depth and reality, not technical writing. Sometimes, this takes practice, but practice away, writers. What is this craft but practice?

• • • •

EXERCISE #34: REVIEW your writing for scenes where you describe movements, and make sure these movements are recorded in ways easy to visualize. Recording "rights" and "lefts" is less important than allowing your reader to see it. Your goal is never to make your reader pause and move their body in echo of your words to figure out exactly what you mean.

You think they won't? Oh, they will. They'll be sitting at a coffee shop reading your book one day, shifting their left arm up and their right fist into an uppercut to make sure they understand your mechanics. But if you distract your reader, pulling them out of your story in a way where they're reconsidering the meaning of your writing, this isn't good.

You want them to turn the pages, not accidentally throw the book when attempting to understand a character's maneuvers.

Question #32:

Did your antagonist "riffle" through your protagonist's house or "rifle" through it?

And does the protagonist have any idea? Are you making your reader nervous? Does the antagonist find what they're looking for?

(Wait, strike those last questions. This editor is just getting excited.)

Empowering Your Dialogue

Dialogue is Not a Screenplay Script

FOR SOME WRITERS, DIALOGUE flows. Maybe you hear your characters talking to you and feel like you are simply the transcriber jotting it all down. Maybe it's brilliant. Maybe it's hilarious. Maybe it's profound. But what it isn't is a screenplay (or at least I'm assuming so since you're reading this novel-editing book).

A novel is a balance of story elements, including dialogue but never only dialogue for long durations of time. Yes, we've talked about ensuring that your characters have unique voices with unique verbal patterns; however, even the best of dialogue cannot stand by itself. If this ever occurs, here is your opportunity to show your characters moving with actions big or small, to insert description and atmosphere. Even a sentence here or a sentence there can balance out a dialogue-heavy scene. A balance of story elements is what makes a novel not only readable but vivid in your reader's mind.

Dialogue should never run for more than a page on its own. Even if it's your favorite part of the writing process, that doesn't mean you can switch to screenplay writing within your novel.

• • • •

EXERCISE #35: AS YOU review your manuscript, if you ever have more than a half-page of dialogue that is not broken up with any surrounding narration, freeze in that scene. Close your eyes. Imagine your characters. Imagine what they do as they talk. Imagine the place where they are. Imagine the emotions of the moment and how they can be conveyed. Imagine the tensions of this scene within your greater plot and how you could intensify it. Now open your eyes and add a little here and a little there as necessary to create a stronger flow and an empowered scene.

Question #33:

Writing crime fiction? What's the past tense of "pleading" guilty? Is it "pled" or "pleaded"?

(You've got to get that pivotal moment in your dialogue right.)

Beware of Awkward Monologues

ARE YOU SOMEONE WHO talks to yourself? Do you talk to yourself a lot? Or maybe I should begin a different way.

Do your characters talk to themselves a lot? Is it an unrealistic amount? First-draft characters seem to talk to themselves more than perhaps they should, like they've memorized a monologue for their time on the stage. Is this realistic? Maybe, maybe not. Does it work for your book? Maybe, maybe not. But think on this. Sometimes readers are distracted by characters who do things more than the average person. Sometimes this is true with something as simple as winking. Are you someone who winks? How many people do you know who wink? Do lots of your characters wink? (Bonus editing tip! Think about your winking.)

Maybe your characters grumble to themselves. Maybe they mumble to themselves. But maybe they do these things too much. Maybe. Only you can decide.

· · · ·

EXERCISE #36: RECONSIDER every instance of a character talking to themselves. Is it realistic? Does it fit naturally? Spend a moment with each instance and decide what's best for every one.

Question #34:

If your protagonist's name is Scott, and if he's not at the party but at home talking to himself, the party might be "Scott-free," but what if he's also getting away with something without punishment? Would he be getting off "scotch-free" or "scot-free"?

Rethink Your Dialogue Tags

THERE'S A SECRET TO dialogue tags: you don't always need them.

What is the point of that "he said" / "she said" / "she asked" / "he whispered" language if your reader clearly already knows who is speaking? Or, if we're really going deep with the idea that every word of your manuscript needs to be there with intention, is this the best usage of your language?

Clarity is essential, but unnecessary words are always worth reexamining. If your dialogue conveys a conversation in a way that only a certain character would speak, you don't need the "Sylvie says" or "Miguel answered." If a conversation within your manuscript is flowing, everyone's turn doesn't need to note their name like a screenplay. Dialogue tags are there for order, nothing more.

And please, writers, think about the word choice of the dialogue tag itself.

"I figured out who the murderer is," she bellowed.
"I'd love to go," she enthused.
"Never again," he croaked.

Where do you want your reader to focus: the words of your dialogue or the dialogue tag itself? If you are too creative with your dialogue tags, they can be distracting to the story. Be careful with your "clucks," your "avows," your "gripes," and so many others. Are any of these words wrong? No. Should you take this as my advice that you should cut them all? Not at all. You are the author of your book. Therefore, you get to dictate what you feel should go there. However, think about how distracting the words you use might be. A simple "said" or "asked" can do just fine. They aren't boring. They're getting the job done without calling attention away from the plot, the characters, and the moment. Or, maybe you don't even need that "said" or "asked" at all.

Here's my favorite method of solving messy dialogue tags: replace the tag with a sentence that captures the speaking character doing something. This strategy enables clarification on who is speaking yet also makes the scene you're writing more vivid, allowing your reader to see your character.

What's more effective?

"What should we do next?" Gloria asked.

or

"What should we do next?" Gloria chopped the carrots so quickly she made everyone else in the room brace themselves for the sight of blood.

"I can't help the way I feel," Calvin said.

or

"I can't help the way I feel." Calvin pushed himself to his feet, making the row-boat rock.

Dialogue tags are a more complicated craft element than they might seem at first glance. What can you do better with yours?

• • • •

EXERCISE #37: YOU CAN search page by page throughout your manuscript or you can search for quotation marks using the "Find" function, but I recommend picking a single chapter with this exercise. I'm going to say lucky chapter seven for the sake of starting you somewhere in the middle for a true experiment, but pick any chapter you'd like if seven doesn't make sense in your manuscript.

Step one, double-check that each spoken word upon your pages is clearly connected with a character. Let's get rid of any lingering confusions.

Step two, review every dialogue tag to ensure the creativity of the words used are not so creative that they distract from the dialogue (the important stuff) itself.

• • • •

EXERCISE #38: FOR THOSE who want to step up their game, examine every usage of "said," "asked," and other dialogue tag choices. Again, the "Find" function is your friend. Where can these tags be cut with no loss? Or if a clarification of a character name is needed, how could you transform that dialogue tag into some-thing that shows your character in the moment instead?

Question #35:

Dialogue is one place you can show a character being "vulnerable," but this is quite different from showing them being "venerable." Do you know the difference?

Cut the Small Talk

DIALOGUE IS SPEECH elevated. It's real, yet it's better than how we speak every day. It's conversation without the small talk and redundancies. It's tightened for literary effect.

Every sentence of dialogue must exist for a reason. Maybe that reason is defining character relationships or illuminating what a character wants or fears. Maybe that dialogue serves a purpose in the greater plot. But do you know what dialogue should not be? It should not be small talk. It should not be all of the repetitive verbal stutters and ums and errs and uhs that occur in everyday speech. You do not need to capture the moment when the drive-through window attendant takes the order, reviews the order, and shares the amount due unless this information is somehow relevant to your story. You do not need to capture the moment where the two characters meet and say "hi" and "how are you?" and "isn't the weather lovely?" unless this conversation is important to your total book.

Think about what comes out of your character's mouth. Dialogue should feel real but intentional.

• • • •

EXERCISE #39: SEEK out your "small talk" and purposeless dialogue. Either make it be there for a reason or cut it entirely. Usually, the best recommendation is the latter.

Question #36:

Dialogue is a great place to tamp down those rumors encircling your protagonist. Or is it to "tap down" those rumors?

Trickle in Unique Descriptions

IMAGINE YOUR CHARACTER walking down a city street. The tension is high. Your story is moving. Do you know what you don't need? A one-page break to talk about the skyscrapers and the wind whipping through the buildings.

But do you know what you absolutely need? Drilled-down atmosphere. A specific beat that will enable your reader to be entirely in the moment and in the exact place with your characters.

Imagine this line in the midst of an emotional argument: "The neon bar sign flickered and buzzed behind her."

Imagine a line like this as a single-sentence breather in between punches thrown: "A cloud of dust swirled, a miniature typhoon between them."

Imagine this sentence right before two characters say goodbye, not knowing if they'll ever see each other again: "Shadows of fish appeared and disappeared in the water underneath the bridge where they stood."

Insert a sentence between lines of dialogue. Add another between character actions. However you do it, the more specific the better, and the more balanced it is with your other story elements, the more organic that description will feel within the scene.

• • • •

EXERCISE #40: EXAMINE the length of your descriptions. Do you have pages where setting and atmosphere are never mentioned? That's like listening to a movie on a blank movie screen. Give us technicolor. No, go further. Give us HD, special effects optional. Add a line or two here and there to bring your story to life.

Or do you have pages where setting and atmosphere go on for lengths that distract from the story? World-building can be powerful, but don't let it distract from your characters or plot. It's all about balance and knowing what your story needs in any given moment. Description is a matter of a happy balance, but little by little is an easy way to weave it in without your readers ever even realizing how fleshed out your fictional world has become.

Question #37:

Should you write about the garden "spicket" or "spigot" with its drip creating a puddle that's big enough to reflect the cloudy April sky?

Cutting the Unnecessary

Capture Your Senses but Not Sensory Words

A GREAT PIECE OF WRITING advice is to use all of your senses when you are describing something. Think about not only the way a place looks but also how it might sound, how it might smell, how it might feel, and yes, even sometimes how something might taste. This level of detail can make a moment, a place, or a world true. But don't delay that description with unnecessary words.

What do I mean by this? I mean phrases that set up the description like "he saw," "she heard," "it smelled like," and "it tasted like." Why do we have to stop and consider the character experiencing the sensation before the detail itself? It's an unnecessary distraction, an unnecessary shift in focus.

You can see the difference in focus and sentence strength:

"She heard the voices from the television in the next room."

vs.

"Voices from the television murmured in the next room."

"He smelled the mint over every other scent of the rooftop garden."

vs.

"The mint overpowered every other scent of the rooftop garden."

If you cut that sensory introduction, that hesitation, the description becomes more direct. You bring your reader straight to it without the stutter-step of bringing your character into the middle of things first. There's nothing wrong with these delays when you write your first draft, when you are still dabbling with ideas throughout your story-writing process. But in the editing stage, it's time for cleanup.

· · · ·

EXERCISE #41: USING your "Find" function, seek out all of your sensory verbs (e.g., look, see, saw, glance, hear, felt, feel, taste, and smell). You can even go a degree further by looking for words like "notice" that also set up descriptions. Consider every use. Would anything be lost if the setup is deleted? Probably not. Chances are that the delete would make the whole stronger.

Note, if you look up "hear," you'll also discover results for "heard." If you look up "notic" (intentional misspelling), you'll get results for "notice," "noticed," and "noticing."

Question #38:

Uh oh, did you encounter a mother load of unnecessary description introductions in your manuscript? Or was it a "mother lode" of them?

Skip the Stalling Words

WHEN I TALK ABOUT WORDS that stall your writing, I'm talking about the wordy words, those unnecessary delays to the actual action of your sentence. Yes, "wordy words" seems obvious—what are words but "wordy"?—but stay with me here.

Maybe a character "starts to" walk. Maybe a character "begins to" move. Maybe a character "is getting ready to" cook their dinner. Maybe someone "is setting out to" solve the puzzle. These words don't add suspense. They just add to the word count.

Using words is good. Using your words well is powerful. By cutting the unnecessary words, you allow your reader to be pulled along faster and sucked in more. And what is your goal as a writer if not to pull your reader into your story?

• • • •

EXERCISE #42: SEARCH for "try," "start," "begin," "set out," and "got ready." Maybe there are even more words you can think of that you use in this way. Examine every instance. What deserves to stay? What can be cut to tighten and strengthen the story?

Question #39:

We've talked about language that slows things down, but let's think about speeding things up. Is your motorcycle-obsessed character "reckless" or "wreckless"?

There's an important difference here.

Question Your Questions in Narration

IT'S YOUR JOB AS A writer to have your readers ask questions and try to figure things out. When you write out a question a character is thinking about, it might be something that the reader is already wondering. And if it's something they are already wondering, it's redundant for you to write it out, isn't it? Don't tell your readers what they should be asking (or what characters are trying to figure out). Simply make them curious and want to turn the next page. Make them ask these questions to themselves.

Many of your characters-thinking-to-themselves questions could be cut with nothing lost. They exist because perhaps they were part of the writing process for you; you were trying to get to the core of these moments. But by the time you finished your first draft, chances are you've already done a wonderful job with making your reader wonder what's going to happen next, including the why and how.

• • • •

EXERCISE #43: USE THE "Find" function and search for question marks. If it sounds like an intimidating exercise, choose any given fifty pages of your book to focus on. Let's say pages 150 through 200. This will give you a large enough sample size to examine. Yes, this will turn up question marks irrelevant to this issue, but keep searching. Chances are, you'll find question marks that apply.

When you find them, ask yourself if your reader is already wondering this question in this moment. If they aren't, how can you cut the question but make them more curious? If they are, debate deleting the question entirely.

Question #40:

Whether you're writing romance or not, are you aware of the difference between "ravish" and "ravage"? Which one means to fill someone with immense delight?

(This is not a typo that will treat you—or your characters—well.)

Avoid Over-Explaining

GIVE YOUR READERS CREDIT. You, as the writer, leave them clues. They are the detectives. It's a wonderfully perfect partnership.

Readers thrive on clues, and I'm not only talking about mystery readers. Readers love being pulled into a story and figuring out what the protagonist is thinking, how this situation has occurred, why people are acting in a certain way, and what the resolution of the problem is going to be. Sometimes writers are so caught up in their own story, they're worried that they're not bringing their reader along well enough. You might be subconsciously troubled over not pulling something off as well as you could. These moments right here are where the over-explaining happens.

Imagine something important has just occurred in your book. Boom. Rather than letting that moment exist for readers to take in and comprehend on their own, are you explaining its importance to your readers, accidentally talking down to them? Give your readers credit. You don't need to hold their hands and explain the significance of what happened.

• • • •

EXERCISE #44: MAKE a list of the major "booms" of your book. Maybe they're action driven. Maybe they're emotionally driven. Whatever they may be, these are the huge turning points. My guess is that you know exactly what they are. Return to those scenes. Where do they stop? Do you discuss them after the fact far longer than you should? Do these discussions bring clarity or repetition of what your reader already knows? If you find these sections, whether in the narration or as a conversation between characters, spend some time with them. Take out your red pen (actual or metaphorical) and respect your reader's ability to keep up.

Question #41:

What's the greater message you want your reader to take away from your story, and is this called the "moral" or the "morale"?

(Of course, you won't bonk your readers on the head with this idea, over-explaining it and making it less powerful, right?)

Consider and Then Reconsider Your Adverbs

DO YOU KNOW WHAT I'M not saying here? I'm not saying to cut every adverb. Instead, I'm recommending that you reconsider every adverb. Some can stay. Many can go. Many should in fact go. But each deserves a moment of extra thought in the editing phase.

Often adverbs are examples of where a writer is being lazy. They are words that allow you to cheat, but don't let yourself cheat. You're better than that. Your readers deserve more.

Don't have a character "say something quietly." Let her "whisper." Don't have a character "move fast." Have them "bolt." Don't have a character "plop down sleepily." Have them blink their eyes, stretch, nestle into their blankets, and hear a lullaby in their mind. The answers are always up to you. Don't let lazy writing weaken your potential.

Adverbs are frequently markers for you, words that are simply killing time, waiting for the language that's out there but not yet captured on the page.

• • • •

EXERCISE #45: SEARCH for "ly" within your manuscript. Will this catch every adverb? Of course not, but it's a surprisingly powerful start. Every time you discover a new adverb, consider how it's used. How could you change your language to make it stronger? How could you evoke the idea? (Ooh, here's that classic "show" versus "tell" advice sneaking in again. Yep, it's classic advice for a reason.)

Question #42:

Are your adverbs "wreaking havoc" or "wrecking havoc"?

Ellipses Are Not Confetti

EVERY TIME YOU USE an ellipsis (...), it is an opportunity to do better—whether you are using it in dialogue to evoke a pause, whether you're using
it within your narration to trail off on a thought, or whatever its purpose might
be ...

(See what I mean? Why do we do that?)

All that ellipsis is doing much of the time is adding confetti to your manuscript. We should not add ticker tape parades to our books to make them better.
I'm kidding, but I'm not.

If you want to evoke a pause within your dialogue, close the quotation mark
and add a single beat—a single sentence—of movement, action, or description. If you would like to trail off on a thought, there are so many other ways
than the haphazard dot-dot-dot that has become ubiquitous across social media, emails, and every other communication that we share. Ellipses are messy.
Are they something to forbid? No. Are they something to rethink? Absolutely.

• • • •

*EXERCISE #46: LOOK at every ellipsis in your manuscript using the handy
"Find" function. Every single one should be considered. Is it messy or serving a true
purpose? Chances are your purpose is better served in another way.*

Question #43:

If your character is feeling ill—or you are, after all of this intense editing work—are they (you?) feeling "nauseated" or "nauseous"?

(Deep breath, writers. You're getting there.)

Avoid Italics-Styled Stumbling Blocks

WHEN YOU WANT TO EMPHASIZE the importance of a word or a line, remember you are a writer, and you have this amazing ability to craft your language with impressive skill. Don't use your font style to cheat the process. Using italics on a word or sentence within your manuscript is not the best way to show the emphasis within a speaker's speech or the importance of an idea.

There can be a time and a place for italics, of course. Perhaps you use them for internal thoughts, for text messages (not quite dialogue but almost), or for countless other reasons. But any moment you feel the need for italics, give it more deliberation. Consider your reader and how they might read that line. Maybe the word that you want to highlight is not the word that your reader would emphasize in a sentence, and that moment of italics is going to be a stumbling block, making them pause and read that line of dialogue again. You never want to make your reader pause and have to read something again.

Or if you're stressing the importance of an idea, why use your font choices for that? Your brilliance and writing talent can shine through without your font backing you up. Have faith in yourself.

• • • •

EXERCISE #47: DO A sweep of your full manuscript looking for when you use italics. If they're used for emphasis, reconsider your strategy.

Question #44:

Why will an editor mark the phrase "thinking to himself/herself" every time?

Scissor Away Extra Words

THE WORDS WE JOT DOWN in our first drafts do not necessarily need to be the words that stick. Sometimes our writing sneaks into warm-up mode, where we use ten words where only two are necessary. Perhaps your character "shrugs their shoulders." Do you really need to write "their shoulders"? What else would they shrug? Perhaps your characters "nod their heads." What else would they nod? Maybe you note that it's "raining outside." Where else would it be raining? A character can "stand" instead of "stand up" and "sit" instead of "sit down."

Take the time to consider your words and whether every one of them is necessary on the page. I realize this is a point you've heard me say before. So maybe these sentences are unnecessary in themselves, and I should cut them—oh, the irony. Think of it as housecleaning, and all of the unnecessary extras are dust motes that can be brushed away.

• • • •

EXERCISE #48: READ your manuscript with a spring-cleaning attitude. (This returns us to the "editing in waves" idea of Exercise #19.) Focus only on this objective for a full pass of a chapter. How many words can you find that are just dust? Clean them away one by one. Then repeat this exercise for every chapter of your book. Daunting? Maybe. But if you want the best, you've got to put in the work. And I know you've got this.

Question #45:

Are you "chomping at the bit" or "champing at the bit" to be finished with this whole editing process?

Micro-Editing Strategies

The "Find" Function

THERE'S ONE TECHNOLOGY trick that you've seen me repeat again and again in this section. We live in a wonderful era. You don't have to slog through your handwritten manuscript to find that one word you know you used somewhere. We live in an era of computers, and this makes the revision process dramatically easier. The "Find" function is an editor's best friend. Learn it. Love it. Discover it among your keyboard's shortcuts (CTRL + F on PCs, Command + F on a Mac).

The "Replace" Function

A WAVE OF SELF-ANNOYANCE can sometimes strike when you realize careless flaws, like too many characters whose names start with the letter A, but this doesn't mean that you need to replace the names one by one in your entire manuscript. You can replace character names with the "Replace" function.

Like the "Find" function for tracking down items within your manuscript, using the "Replace" function (CTRL + H on PCs and Macs) can make your life so much easier. Every "Alice" could become "Suri" at the click of a button. It's magic. Say what you want about technology and its place in our world, but it is a writer's best friend in many ways.

However, be aware if your character name (new or old) may exist within other words of your manuscript. Replacing "Ann" with "Lydia" may sound simple, but then there's a chance you'll have words like "annual" and "unannounced" that become "Lydiaual" and "unLydiaounced." Replacing " Ann" with " Lydia" will help with some of this. (Do you see the single space used in front of the replaced terms?) This way, only usages of Ann with a space in front of it will be replaced—no more "unLydiaounced"!—but it's still an imperfect method when it comes to false replacements like "Lydiaual." Other Anns might still be hiding. This, among so many other tiny details, is where that final proofing comes in.

• • • •

EXERCISE #49: (BONUS Micro-Editing Exercise!): Take a moment to consider the names of your characters. Do any of them sound similar? Could any of them be easily confused? Do many of them start with the same letter? Make sure you're not setting up character names that are unnecessarily confusing for your readers.

Question #46:

Yep, we're finally turning to proofreading. Would you say just in the "nick of time" or just in the "knick of time"?

Proofreading

EVEN THOUGH YOU HAVE read your novel manuscript a gazillion times, that does not mean that you have caught every error. Before you call your work "done," you must do that final proofread. This is a different editing stage than your macro-edit or your micro-edit. This is your final sweep, detail-oriented and precision-focused. This is where every last punctuation mark should be corrected and every last typo should be caught.

Yes, you might hand your book off to an editor, agent, or publisher, but your job—as the writer—is to not just take it most of the way. You need to take it as far as you possibly can, and that includes the proofreading, the last opportunity to make your manuscript shine.

Question #47:

True or False: "A" always goes before words that start with a consonant, and "an" always goes before words that start with a vowel.

Read Your Work Aloud

SO OFTEN OUR BRAINS know what we want to say, but that idea does not always transfer from our heads down our necks out our shoulders across our arms and to our fingertips typing on the keyboard. When you know exactly what you meant to say, in the proofreading stage, your eyes might quickly skim over mistakes.

When you read your work aloud, your ears and voice enable you to hear your work in a new way, making you a stronger editor. This exercise takes more time and more concentration, but when you read things aloud, your ears will catch a subject-verb mistake or an awkward line, a character whose name isn't correct or a plot inconsistency. Your ear is an amazing editor.

And let's even take this one step further. Technology gives us some pretty amazing editorial tools, and I don't only mean "Find" and "Replace" functions. Many software programs—hey there, Microsoft Word—can now read your text aloud to you. It's a bit like a novice audiobook production, but you know your computer won't let you get away with things. It could make that wrong word obvious (when a character "defiantly" does something rather than "definitely" doing it). It could make that wordy sentence blatantly clear.

Your computer's voice does not yet have the ability to correct things, so take advantage of this moment in technology history.

• • • •

EXERCISE #50: READ your work aloud or have your computer read it to you. If you have a small child who is practicing their reading and your book is appropriate for them, have them read it aloud. Use this exercise for friend and family bonding if you dare to be brave. However you choose to do it is up to you.

Question #48:

When someone says something nice about your finished book, is this a "compliment" or "complement"?

Reread Your Book in a New Form

LITERALLY SEEING YOUR book in a new way is a highly recommended final proofing strategy. When you print it out or change its digital form, it triggers your brain to see this text as something new and different. You don't have to be so eco-unfriendly. You can print two-sided papers with multiple pages printed on both sides of the sheet if you'd like. Or, if you're choosing to make these changes on a screen, change the font of your manuscript for this final proofing. Better yet, save the manuscript as an .epub file or as a .pdf and read it on your tablet or smartphone.

However you do it, be sure to give yourself a fresh look at this work that you have spent countless hours, days, weeks, months, and years on.

• • • •

EXERCISE #51: CHANGE the way your manuscript appears—whether you look at it on paper or in a new way on your favorite device. Then read it again with a focus on precision.

Question #49:

After staring at your manuscript for so long, is your vision getting "blurry" or "bleary"?

(Hopefully, neither, but if this were the case, which would it be?)

Edit Backward

LET ME INTRODUCE YOU to the editing tip that makes writers groan every time I share it: read your work backward.

Now, what do I mean by "backward"? Do I mean word-by-word backward? Absolutely not. That's absurd, painful sounding, and perhaps a writer torture project. What I mean is that in the final proofing stage, if you have every other piece of your work in amazing order, you should consider reading your project backward sentence by sentence. Yes, go to the very last sentence of your book, read that last sentence to double-check for any grammar mistakes or typos, and then—after you read that sentence—read the second to last sentence, then the third to last sentence, and on and on.

Why do I even suggest an idea that might sound like torture to poor writers who are simply trying to finish their books? Think on this for a moment. When you edit your own work, you know the story so well, and there always comes a point where you forget to keep on your editing hat. Suddenly, you're pulled in. You have that paragraph you are so proud of. You are a writer rock star. You nailed that scene. Your profundity is amazing. The emotional truth in that moment is inspiring. You're loving this project. But you're no longer editing it. You're reading it.

It's hard not to fall into the rhythm of being a reader, even when you're focused on your editing. However, when you read backward, you can't be sucked into reading your story. You force yourself to pay attention line by line—the spelling, the word choices, the punctuation, and all those nitty-gritty little things that matter.

So yes, I highly recommend this exercise. I hear you groaning somehow through the pages of this book, but do it. You'll see its power if you do.

• • • •

EXERCISE #52: READ your work backward sentence by sentence. Pay attention to the details. Find all the remaining imperfections.

Question #50:

Are you having visions of your readers "fawning" all over you? Or is it "fauning" all over you?

Never Edit More Than Ten Pages (or Ten Minutes) at a Time

EDITING REQUIRES FOCUS, and this is especially true when you work on your own manuscript. How many times have you read through your novel? Maybe you don't want to answer that question. And that's okay. But when you dive deep into your editing work, especially when you're going page by page, sentence by sentence, forward or backward, our eyes and our brains get tired.

Maybe you smile at a wonderful line. Maybe you laugh hysterically at your own hilarity. Maybe your heart beats and your body clenches with fear or heat or anger. But whether you've fallen into a pattern of reading or whether you've fallen into a moment of distraction, you know what you're not doing in those moments? Editing.

Try to keep yourself in check every paragraph and every page, but give your-self a time or page limit where you force yourself to take a break. Your brain needs it. Your break can be as simple as standing up. Look away from your screen. Go pour yourself a glass of water. Your body probably needs that hydra-tion anyway. It does not need to be a big pause, but you need to get your mind to look at something else for a moment.

If you don't give yourself these respites, there will come a point in your edit-ing process that you start reading. Maybe that point won't happen on page ten. (We always have a great attention span for the start-of-the-book edits, don't we?) Maybe that point won't happen on page fifty, even—Go, you, if your edit-ing attention span holds strong!—but there's always that point when your brain becomes fatigued and sloppy. Take your breaks before you need them so your editing doesn't suffer.

• • • •

EXERCISE #53: SET A timer for ten minutes. Work on your proofreading, but when the alarm goes off, stand up. Touch your toes or stretch your arms out; walk across the room; touch the opposite wall; walk back to your computer; sit back down, and go for it.

If you dare to use social media as your break, that's fine too, but set a timer for yourself on that as well. Give yourself five minutes, no more. Then jump back into your editing.

Question #51:

Are all of these editing tricks and tips going to take your writing "further" or "farther"?

When to Hire an Editor

EVEN AFTER YOU SPEND the time to do thorough editing work, your mind can still trick you. I know it seems almost unfair after all of that work. But it's true. You might not notice that stray comma because of the speck of dust on your screen, or who knows why certain things still slip through the cracks?

Everyone—let me repeat this: everyone—needs to have eyes that are not their own on their book before it is published. If you plan on going the indie publishing route, don't cut corners and skip this step. Self-published books don't have the stigma that they once did; however, that stigma is there largely because of a lack of good editing.

This question comes up every time I speak and there's a Q & A session, so let me end with it right here.

Do you need an editor for your manuscript?

Maybe.

Okay, so that's not an answer that is as clear-cut as you want it to be. Here's what might help, though:

Have you taken the time to bring your manuscript to the most polished state possible, doing the work yourself first to ensure your narrative structure, characters, plot logic, voice, pacing, and word choice are all as powerful as they can be? Has your manuscript been through a critique partner or beta readers who have given you notes besides the fact that they "are proud of you" or that "it's really good"? We all need those "it's really good" readers, but they don't help a book along its journey.

Every manuscript can get better. DaVinci said that art is never finished; it is only abandoned. And this is oh-so-true when it comes to writing.

You need an editor if you have done everything you can do, but you feel like you still need help.

You need an editor if you don't know how to accomplish what you need to accomplish.

You need an editor if you plan on self-publishing your work. And that is the one time I will say hands down that an editor is one hundred percent necessary.

You need an editor if your query or pitch is doing well, but your submitted pages aren't quite closing the deal.

Editing isn't easy. I believe we've covered that here. Writers need to take it upon themselves to begin the heavy-lifting on their own, but when your revision muscles begin to quiver and you aren't sure if you can make it much further, freelance editors are available reinforcements ready to help.

Be aware that editors have different specialties, including macro-editing services like developmental edits and manuscript critiques, micro-editing services like copyediting or substantive editing, and even proofreading services like line-editing. If you are someone who sees an editor in your future, be aware of these different levels of editing and be sure you know which one your book needs. So many writers approach editors for the final proofread when there's still some big macro- and micro-editing work to be done.

Patience. Determination. A meticulous work ethic like no one even realizes. Writers are on a journey that requires fortitude. Finding the right editor to help your project (or your career) should be a decision as important as any other. Ask for client testimonials. Schedule a time to chat about your project, your needs, their interests, their process, and all of the business details (like costs and timing) before anything is decided.

Editorial partnerships can be powerful, but it's a relationship like any other. You need to find the fit that works best for you. Every writer's situation is different, just like every writer's process is different. There is no easy answer to any of this, but editorial eyes that are impartial—not emotionally attached to your body of work—can be valuable. Maybe it's a professional editor. Maybe it's a fellow writer in your local writing community or a genre-specific organization you've joined. But whoever it is, make sure your novel goes through someone else's hands before you call it officially "done."

Also remember that editors might not be the only extra eyes your manuscript needs. If any of your characters come from backgrounds different from your own, take the time to find an authenticity reader—also called a sensitivity reader—to ensure that you're not accidentally stumbling into stereotypes or culturally insensitive areas. We don't always know what we don't know. Partnerships can help in so many ways.

Question #52:

Does the editing process make you feel like you've
been put through the "ringer" or the "wringer"?

You've Got This

HOW MANY OF THE FIFTY-THREE editing exercises did you tackle with your novel manuscript? And after you've done some of the revision work, can you see the difference? Heck yeah, you can. Look at that novel getting closer and closer to that book you dreamed it could be. Take it in, writer. Own it. You are making it happen.

Do you need to follow every piece of guidance in this workbook? Of course not. Do you know who the author of your book is? That would be you. But taking the time to reconsider every choice enables you to make your story and your language use intentional. We should have more thoughtfully considered, intentional language in the world, right?

In the eighteenth century, Jean-Jacques Rousseau claimed that it was impossible to be fully understood via written communication. He claimed there would always be miscommunications, misunderstandings, and ideas that wouldn't be able to be conveyed fully. You know what I say? Keep going. Keep editing. I have faith you can bring your project to exactly the place it needs to be.

You had the dream. You did the work. You're getting there. You've got this.

Answers

1. Why shouldn't you talk about your "fictional novel"? It's redundant. A "novel," by definition, is fiction. Be careful not to sound naïve about your work.

2. If you want to build upon a new concept, do you want to "flesh out" or "flush out" your idea? You want to "flesh it out," like you're putting meat on a skeleton of an idea.

3. Is it time to "dive" in or "delve" in? Maybe both could apply, but do you know the difference? For the purposes of our discussion, to "dive in" means to plunge into something or to begin. To "delve in" means to dig in, whether with a shovel or with an inquisitive mind, analyzing something closely. There are more definitions, but these address the question at hand.

4. Is your character going through a "right" of passage, a "rite" of passage, or a "write" of passage? This may or may not apply to your story, but knowing the right word is still worth it. A "rite of passage" is a moment or ritual that acts as a crossover to a new stage of life. This is usually what a writer is looking for. A "right of passage" doesn't come up nearly as much as the first, but it could refer to the ability or permission to cross through a certain territo-ry.

5. Are you trying to "shore up" or "sure up" your plot? The correct expression is "to shore up." "To sure up" is a common typo.

6. If you want to send a character's dog after a villain, would you "sic" the dog or "sick" the dog on them? You would "sic" the dog on them.

7. Is a villain planning on "extracting revenge" or "exacting revenge"? To "exact revenge" is the correct wording.

8. Let's talk "heroine" vs. "heroin." Which one is the drug, and which one is the female lead of a story? A "heroine" is a female hero. "Heroin" is a drug.

9. What is the plural of "passerby"? Passersby.

10. Do you have a character who might "nash," "knash," or "gnash" his or her teeth? Or is this editing process making you do it? (I hope not!) The correct spelling is to "gnash" your teeth.

11. Is your character not "phased" by another's action or not "fazed" by it? One isn't "fazed" by another's action. The moon might have "phases," but that's not what you're looking for here.

12. If a character is in a stage of difficulty, are they "in the throws" of something or "in the throes" of it? The correct expression is "in the throes."

13. If your character is trying to figure something out, are they "poring" over their research books or "pouring" over them? The correct wording is "poring," as in to intensely study.

14. If you have a character who is trying their best to be patient, are they waiting with "baited breath" or "bated breath"? The correct expression is "bated" breath. Unless they are an impatient fish, of course.

15. If you, as the writer, missed something that you now realize you should return to, would you say you "passed up the opportunity" or "past up the opportunity" to fully tackle that moment in your earlier drafts? The correct spelling would be "passed up."

16. If you mention the details of a character's apartment that show-case how it's decorated to suit their personality, would you talk about the "flair" of the space or "flare" of it? "Flair" means style. "Flare" relates to flames, so here's hoping you mean the first!

17. This editing process takes time, but sometimes you have to "grin and bear it." Or is it "grin and bare" it? You want "grin and bear it" un-less you're losing some clothing. Yikes!

18. If you're working on an updated version of a previously published book, is it a second "addition" or a second "edition"? A new "edition" of a book is a significantly updated version of it.

19. Does this editing process make you want to "hunker down" or "bunker down"? Or at least answer this: what's the correct version of this phrase? To "hunker down" is the correct phrase.

20. Is that project you're working on a "work-in-progress" or a "work-in-process"? ("#wip" won't help you with this one.) "Work-in-progress" is the standard form.

21. Button down the hatches, writers. Things are about to get intense! Or should you "batten" them down? "Batten down the hatches" is the correct wording.

22. Did your character's grandmother "instill" values or "install" values in your character? Unless your character is a robot, android, or similar cyborg, you're looking for the word "instill."

23. Should I say, "Every once and a while," you might be able to get away with these wordings, or should I say, "Every once in a while," you could do it? "Every once in a while" is the standard form.

24. If you're bringing your reader into a past time period, are you writing "historic" or "historical" fiction? "Historical" refers to the past. "His-toric" refers to something in the past that was world-changing in some way. "Historical fiction" is the genre name.

25. Your editing work should run the gamut from big-picture revision to proofreading for the tiniest of details. Or should it run the "gambit"? Or should it run the "gauntlet"? If you're looking for the expression referring to covering the whole spectrum, you're looking for "runs the gamut."

26. Should a character have a nervous "tick" or a nervous "tic"? A sudden movement or personal mannerism is a "tic." A worried arachnid is a "nervous tick."

27. Should you write about a hungover character waking up feeling "grisly" or "grizzly"? Unless they are a bear, it should be "grisly."

28. Your character might just have realized their plan isn't working. Should they "change tact" or "change tack"? They should "change tack."

29. Think fast: is it "all of the sudden" or "all of a sudden"? "All of a sudden" is the correct form of this phrase.

30. Do you know the difference between being "uninterested" and "disinterested"? Some might be uninterested in all of these craft subtleties, but you, storyteller, are officially bringing your A game. Being "uninterested" means you don't care. Being "disinterested" means you're impartial, not feeling strongly in one way or the other.

31. Does your protagonist do too much "naval-gazing"? Or is it "navel-gazing"? Self-absorbed introspection is referred to as "navel-gazing."

32. Did your antagonist "riffle" through your protagonist's house or "rifle" through it? "To rifle" means to quickly search, which makes more sense in this context.

33. Writing crime fiction? What's the past tense of "pleading" guilty? Is it "pled" or "pleaded"? Contrary to what popular television shows might use, the standard past tense of "plead" is actually "pleaded." However, be-cause "pled" has gained such popularity and has a history of common usage, it is also considered acceptable in many situations. As for your book? I'd recommend "pleaded," the standard usage.

34. If your protagonist's name is Scott, and if he's not at the party but at home talking to himself, the party might be "Scott-free," but what if he's also getting away with something without punishment? Would he be getting off "scotch-free" or "scot-free"? "Scot-free" is the correct phrase.

35. Dialogue is one place you can show a character being "vulnerable," but this is quite different from showing them being "venerable." Do you know the difference? Someone "vulnerable" is in a state where they could be easily wounded (emotionally or physically); someone "venerable" is highly respected.

36. Dialogue is a great place to tamp down those rumors encircling your protagonist. Or is it to "tap down" those rumors? To "tamp down" rumors is the correct usage.

37. Should you write about the garden "spicket" or "spigot" with its drip creating a puddle that's big enough to reflect the cloudy April sky? The standard spelling is "spigot."

38. Uh oh, did you encounter a "mother load" of unnecessary description introductions in your manuscript? Or was it a "mother lode" of them? "Mother lode" is the correct form of this phrase.

39. We've talked about language that slows things down, but let's think about speeding things up. Is your motorcycle-obsessed character "reckless" or "wreckless"? There's an important difference here. "Reckless" means wild and uninhibited; "wreckless" isn't a word, but if it were, I imagine it would mean without any wrecks.

40. Whether you're writing romance or not, are you aware of the difference between "ravish" and "ravage"? Which one means to fill someone with immense delight? This is not a typo that will treat you (or your characters) well. "To ravish" is to enrapture, fill with delight, or carry someone off by force; "to ravage" is to devastate or destroy.

41. What's the greater message you want your reader to take away from your story, and is this called the "moral" or the "morale"? The "moral" of the story is the takeaway lesson.

42. Are your adverbs "wreaking havoc" or "wrecking havoc"? The correct expression is "to wreak havoc."

43. If your character is feeling ill, is she feeling "nauseated" or "nauseous"? "Nauseated" is actually the correct word here. Please, please, please learn the difference.

44. Why will an editor mark up the phrase "thinking to himself" every time? Let me answer this question with a question. Is it possible to think to anyone else but one's self? Unless your novel involves telepathy, the "to himself" and "to herself" language can be cut here every time.

45. Are you "chomping at the bit" or "champing at the bit" to be finished with this whole editing process? The correct phrase is "champing at the bit."

46. Would you say just in the "nick of time" or just in the "knick of time"? The correct phrase includes the "nick" of time.

47. True or False?: "A" always goes before words that start with a consonant, and "an" always goes before words that start with a vowel. False. It's more about the first sound than the first letter. "A unicorn" and "an honor" are both correct.

48. When someone says something nice about your finished book, is this a "compliment" or "complement"? A kind word is a "compliment."

49. After staring at your manuscript for so long, is your vision getting "blurry" or "bleary"? Hopefully, neither, but if this were the case, which would it be? "Blurry" would make more sense when thinking about how something is seen. "Bleary" means tired or exhausted.

50. Are you having visions of your readers "fawning" all over you? Or is it "fauning" all over you? "Fawning" can be a verb, as in to dote up-on someone. "Faun" is only a noun, as in a mythical creature with the legs and horns of a goat (usually a goat, anyhow). Thus, here's hoping your readers will fawn all over you.

51. Are all of these editing tricks and tips going to take your writing "further" or "farther"? They will take your writing "further." "Farther" only applies if there's a measurable distance involved. An editor on a train might take your work both further and farther.

52. Does the editing process make you feel like you've been put through the "ringer" or the "wringer"? The correct expression is to be put through the "wringer."

For more English language and storytelling reminders like these, sign up for Kris Spisak's monthly newsletter at **Kris-Spisak.com.**

Also by Kris Spisak:

Get a Grip on Your Grammar:
250 Writing and Editing Reminders for the Curious or Confused
(Career Press, 2017)

"Is it a dash or a colon here? Should I write first person or third? Is it 'already' or 'all ready'? In this handy manual, grammar guru Kris Spisak offers us her thoughts and tips on the writing questions that dog every writer's life. You'll want to keep a copy on your desk."
- *Meg Medina, Newbery and Pura Belpré Award winning author*

"*Get a Grip on Your Grammar* is not only a useful reference. It's also a fun read, chock-full of telling examples and pop-culture references."
- *Charles Euchner, author of* Keep It Short: A Practical Guide to Writing in the 21st Century; *former lecturer on writing, Yale University*

"I know about as much about grammar as I do about kite surfing, but Kris Spisak's delightful, breezy take has dark powers that give a rookie like me fingers instead of left thumbs, light instead of fog."
- *Kevin Smokler, Author of* Brat Pack America: A Love Letter to 80s Teen Movies *(Rare Bird Books, 2016)*

Available wherever books are sold.

Editing Notes:

CPSIA information can be obtained
at www.ICGtesting.com
Printed in the USA
FSHW011735290120
66571FS

9 781734 452402